NHL icehockey worldwide indiany

AF273245

Peter Oberfrank – Hunziker

Impressum:

Bibliografische Information der Deutschen Nationalbibliothek: Die Deutsche Nationalbibliothek verzeichnet diese Publikation in der Deutschen Nationalbibliografie; detaillierte bibliografische Daten sind im Internet über www.dnb.de abrufbar.

© 2022 Peter Oberfrank – Hunziker
Herstellung und Verlag
BoD – Books on Demand, Norderstedt

ISBN 9783837119341

My written worldwide journeying indiany book by me Peter Oberfrank – Hunziker with the booktiteling „NHL icehockey worldwide indiany" is a great sporty book with NHL festivals and hearty indiany and great creative ceremonying.

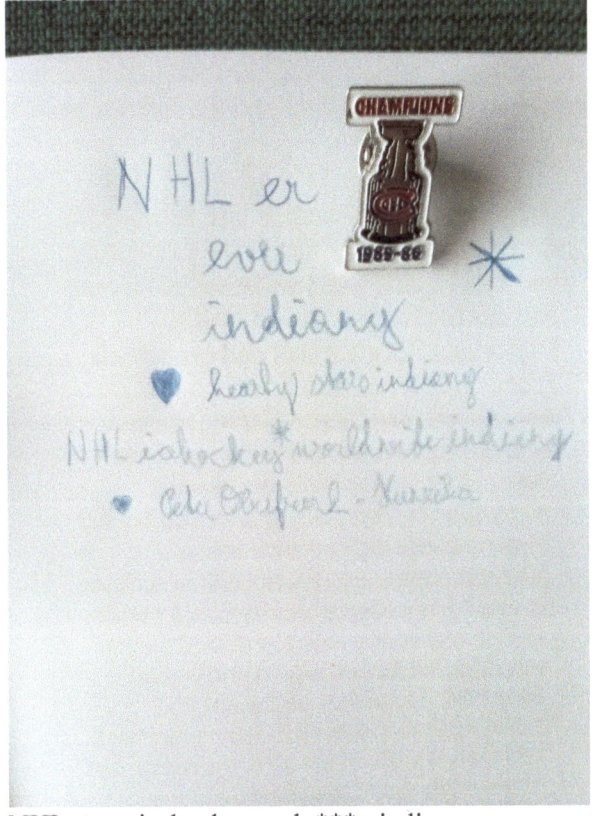

NHL stars icehockeygoal *** indiany

creative NHL ceremonying indiany is me Peter Oberfrank - Hunziker being with all my NHL art naming and being really with joy and smiling and being unique indiany Peter Oberfrank - Hunziker

NHL icehockey indiany is me being Peter Oberfrank - Hunziker with all my NHL art naming and NHL Stanley cup champions with all NHL teams ever and captainying ever all NHL teams and NHL ist the best and highest icehockey League and stands for National Hockey League and Nature History League and National History League with worldwide indiany stars festivals and me Peter Oberfrank - Hunziker being with my family Hunziker with my beauty weddingly Michelle Hunziker and our five funny children indianyly Miri and Tiri and Liri and Amelie and Linea and I Peter Oberfrank - Hunziker am NHL icehockey player ever and technical workying ever and true in heart being and and unique indiany being and being manly ever and sportying ever and funny partying indiany Peter Oberfrank - Hunziker

Today on 16th February 2022 I Peter Oberfrank –
Hunziker celebrate my NHL american indiany
happy sportying indiany festival ever and
remembering all journeying with my family and
great being with all my NHL art.

happy celebrating
indiany

blue festivalying indiany

NHL trainingscamp and great sportying with icehockey training and sportsgymnastic and running and NHL partying and dancing and shaking and funny partying and NHL interview zone and NHL cultural award celebrating indiany and smily indiany ☺

All 32 NHL teams

New York Rangers
NHL icehockeyshield
Great NHL icehockeygame team New York Rangers versus against nature land Suddetelar altc sudetendeutsche and great icehockeyfestival in New York Madison Square Garden with NHL Fanfaren and great winning for my NHL team New York Rangers with me ever captainying with my original name Peter Oberfrank – Hunziker and my NHL art naming liking 99 Wayne Gretzky and great scored highligthning icehockeygoal in the right over angle and great icehockeypuck in the goal scored great in 59 minutes and 59 seconds and great international NHL partying indiany *
NHL book festival
NHL all star indiany wordwide festival indiany
St. Patrick church festivalying hearty indiany

7

NHL skyblue indiany

NHL New York Rangers jerseying and celebrating
indiany

NHL superior pocali New York Rangers indiany

NHL creative icehockey and scoring
icehockeygoal indiany

New York Islanders
Islanders are highlanders

Hitstar party indiany
Bubble party indiany

Tampa Bay Lightning
My great also NHL team with me Peter Oberfrank
– Hunziker ever captainying with my NHL art
naming like NHL 79 Ross Colton and great
indiany NHL icehockeyteam as NHL Stanley Cup
champions in year 2021 and celebrating with all
NHL teams in League association and Lightning is
highlighnting indiany ***
I Peter Oberfrank – Hunziker scored with my NHL
art naming like 79 Ross Colton in glancefully
worldwide sports arena in NHL Stanley Cup Final
year 2021 in second period and 13 minutes and 27
seconds a playfull clinching icehockeygoal to the
winning of the NHL Stanley Cup Trophy in year
2021 and in Tampa Bay is Ligthning ever indiany
celebrating indiany

****

Indiany

great celebrating NHL Stanley Cup champions in
year 2021 my team Tampa Bay Lightning

easy
highlightning
indiany

NHL great perthalerlen at Alpensee indiany

NHL team Canada celebrating olympics gold
medal with highlevelling icehcokey
NHL star 87 Sydney Crosby penguins partying
indiany
Olympic partying
NHL team Pittsburgh Penguins
indiany partying

Montreal Canadiens
NHL champions icehockey indiany

Toronto Maple Leafs

NHL Toronto star

New Jersey Devils
NHL icehockey party american indiany
russian store indiany and american indiany living
style indiany

Chicago Blackhawks
creative indiany
NHL tampylen parties indiany

Buffalo Sabres
Berlin arena O2 NHL festivals and sportying
indiany and HSV Hamburger Sportverein festivals
and CSKA sportying association winning festival
indiany

Columbus Blue Jackets
Kappa jacket
Rapidlauf
stars gaming icehockey and grande ceremonying
international indiany

Washington Capitals
WOW indiany   8 Ovechkin
NHL Washingtoni
indiany

star party indiany

Calgary Flames
NHL star festival

Rapperswil parties indiany

Ottawa Senators
cheerio

Philadelphia Flyers
ceremonying indiany

Detroit Red Wings
Detroity contracting ever indiany
NHL Piratenschiff party indiany

Anaheim Ducks
NHL Ducks museum

Florida Panthers
great NHL partying and surfing indiany

Vancouver Canucks
Island living indiany

Nashville Predators
music festivals

Dallas Stars
indiany stars
funny NHL partying Pavelski indiany festivalying
stars indiany

green parties
indiany parties
stars parties
indiany

Austrian parties

Hip Hop parties

dancing parties

Hippie parties

NHL beach parties

nhly indiany

NHL superpotying indiany

Winnipeg Jets
fashion indiany museum

Minnesota Wild Stars
great farm team Iowa Wild   indiany
NHL trainingscenter and sportying worldwide
NHL marketing indiany

Seattle Kraken
icehockeypartying indiany
great winning party and NHL Fanfaren music

easy nature festivals and sporty festivals indiany
and cultural festivals and NHL museum party
indiany

Los Angeles Kings
kings partying indiany
Indianerschlumpf
kingsy
indiany
NHL party fashion clothing indiany show indiany
nature festival
history museum
beachying
holidaying
icehockeyying

Arizona Coyotes
dschungel parties indiany

NHL icehockey worldwide indiany

Las Vegas Golden Knights
great NHL parties in the nights and celebrating
indiany

glitter city festivals and indiany glitter

indiany

San Jose Sharks
art musem

Boston Bruins   NHL stars icehockeygoal
NHL partying indiany

woody museum and Woodywoodpecker parties
indiany

great NHL stars party indiany

Colorado Avalanche
NHL Presidents Trophy Champions in year 2021
with me ever captainying also my NHL team in
League association with my NHL art naming like
Nathan McKinnon

Edmonton Oilers
NHL 99 Wayne Gretky icehockeyfestival
Edmonti
NHL parties Oilers are Hoilers

indiany

NHL team Carolina Hurricanes
indiany celebrating with NHL jersey canes

VfB Stuttgart ceremonying
great running

NHL indiany

NHL team St. Louis Blues
indiany NHL icehockeygoal
NHL presenting ever and great NHL series ever
and familiary being indiany

Confetti party and NHL museum visiting indiany
and great ever NHL icehockeysport celebrating
indiany

NHL all star indiany

NHL jersey blue indiany festivalying indiany

NHL ever stars indiany is for me Peter Oberfrank -
Hunziker as NHL icehockeyplayer ever and
technical working ever and NHL Stanley Cup
champions ever with all NHL teams and being
with all my NHL art naming like 24 Perthaler and

17 Rem Murray and NHL Ottawa Senators and NHL Network and einzigartig and jury and NHL conference and Prosit and NHL Washington academy and skyblue and strict rules and NHL trophies indiany and smily and true in heart being and laughing and dancing fashion clothing and NHL 19 Steven Yzerman

and Heatley

and Dury

and all sports indiany

and Diego Armando Maradona and Hansi Müller
and Alberto Tomba and Ingemar Stenmark and
Zico and Zidane and Kevin Keegan and football
festivals and sportsgymnastic and Aerobic and
Yoga and sporty gymnastic indiany and Sampras
and Nadal and Agassi and Miller and Tom Brady
and Stafford and LA Rams and Tampa Bay
Buccaneers and Kansas City Chiefs and New York
Yankees and Harlem Globetrotters and Los
Angeles Lakers and Milwaukee Bucks and Werder
Bremen and Philadelphia 76 ers and Mario
Kempes and team Argentina and football Brasil
and calcio Italy and Vialli and Rossi and Bruno
Pezzey and Rodax and Raul Nestor Pipo Gorosito
and Argentina football party indiany   ****

and Nödl and austrian partying indiany
Philadelphia street festivals

and KAC
NHL player Cards parties indiany

and draft and signing and NHL partying indiany and 20 Henrique Lundqvist and 99 Wayne Gretzky and NHL Joe Thornton and 71 Isbister and NHL New York Islanders cappy indiany and nhly and kingsy and 4 Belland and Yevgeni Malkin and Krutov and artist and international icehockeyplayer and NHL 88 Vasilvesky and Pietrangelo and great staring and Goudet and Atzteka football estadio and Rockefeller Center and NHL zertifikat and great running and Australia Day run and NHL sportying indiany and team Canada and 87 Sydney Crosby

and 26 Thomas Vanek and Detroity and 88
Vasilveskiy and 91 Steven Stamkos and Pat
Maroon and 98 Mikhail Sergachev

and all books festival ISBN 9783837028324
NHL fanfaren
team olympic
Devils star indiany

sportying indiany
nhling indiany

and NHL referees and NHL board and NHL
television and Austria Wien Fußballklub mit guten
Wiener Schmäh juhäh glancefull Fußball

and NHL happy joyy and 16 Lavallee and Pertl and
presenting ever and newyorkrangers and
weddingly and NHL winterwonderlandy and all
sports and manly ever and 8 Ovechkin and NHL
Washinhton Capitals Washingtoni and glancefully
and NHL great perthalerlen at Alpensee indiany
and creative indiany celebrating indiany and ewigi
indiany and unique and family Hunziker and
remembering and indiany and NHL er ever indiany
stars indiany hearty stars indiany NHL icehockey
stars worldwide indiany and NHL 79 Ross Colton
and all my art and NHL tampy happy stars indiany
and all sports and Pavelski and NHL museum and
NHL shop and NHL player cards and Devils and
NHL jerseying and NHL festivalying and NHL
worldwide journeying indiany and NHL Dallas
stars indiany and NHLY Montreal Canadiens and
indiany sign and trainingscenter and NHL
superpotying indiany and NHL creative
icehockeysportscenter indiany and
celebrationcenter indiany

and NHL fashion music party Musical operas
cinema cheerio festivalying indiany

and NHL Philadelphia Flyers indiany

and NHL tampy parties indiany

and 28 Claude Giroux and Backes and NBA and
FIFA and NFL and sports trophy indiany and NHL
Weihnachtsbuch and NHL clothing and NHL Mc
Donalds and good eating and drinking and buildy
indiany and Gösser EV and Werner Kerth and
Stockman and Coca Cola parties indiany and
Kappa and ranking ever and NHL series and Iowa
Wild indiany and newyorky and NHL St. Louis
Blues great icehockey indiany and Washington
capitol and Pueblo and grauschwarzglanzig and
NHL Las Vegas Golden Knights star and HSV

and spacy indiany

and indiany creative sign

and Belland parties

celebrating icehockeystars indiany

NHL joyfull indiany

and NHL museumary

and NHL pin

and NHL cheerio pin

and NHLY presenting ever
all stars NHL worldwide indiany

MTV Coca Cola report indiany

and creative indiany and NHL 61 Rick Nash icehockeyshow indiany and NHL confetti partying indiany and NHL cinema indiany and NHL palmosly indiany and Confetti show indiany and NHLY happy indiany and great sportying and Admira Wacker and Graz 99ers and sehr genau and very accurate and stars partying indiany and cooking and fashionying and easy and NHL gardening and NHL Madison Square Garden indainy and NHL icehockey gaming indiany and thinking and NHL jersesys festival indiany and

and Kaapo Kakko

and Lemieux

and NHL Maskottchen
and Rapid Bärli
and NHL trainingssuit
and happy partying
indiany

stars indiany

pingerlen festivals

happy clowning inidany

and nfl touchdown

Los Angeles partying
dancing and fashion style
NHL kingsy icehockey

*

and joky indiany

and 66 Marc Messier

and NHL icehockeyplayer 93 Mika Zibanejad
and me Peter Oberfrank – Hunziker being happy
daddy indiany

WU 59 indiany

and Washington castle indiany

and 47 NHL player Martin St. Louis

tampy parties indiany

and NHL Stanley Cup parties indiany

and NHL star icehockeyplayer Jaromir Jagr
NHL academy   indiany

NHL icehockey worldwide indiany

NHL ever celebrating indiany

and NHL museum historical and

NHL joking indiany

jogging

gardening

singing

dancing

creative being

NHL 77 Hedman
NHL 86 Kucherov

indiany tampylen indiany

Lego playing with my familiary kids
indiany
Hunzi
indiany

and russian international NHL icehockeyplayer
Sergei Makarov

NHLY

NHL icehockeyparty worldwide indiany
stars indiany

and Eric Lindros NHL icehockeystar indiany

NHL snowboardskateboarding indiany

ceremony hall

Hall of fame

NHL dreaming and being indiany

sleeping

calm

activity

palying

smiling

laughing

thinking after

creative

unique

NHL lila festivalying indiany

calm

NHL festival parties indiany

ECR festivals

EHC Black wings Linz

NHL wingerlen festeln indiany

HC Bozen Südtirol

südtirolerisch reden

Ein netter Südtiroler Witz gut Fußball spielen in
der Sommerhitz und schön feiern mit den Music
Party Hits und sportlich trainieren und jubelieren
und im Winter super Eishockey spielen und
gewinnen und mit guten italienischen Festival
zelebrieren.

„HC Tiroler Wasserkraft Innsbruck – Die Haie"

Anthony Cirelli festival with Rockstar partying indiany

Olympic center

NHL grande presenting ever

indiany

NHL ever stars indiany and NHL olympic indiany
Peter Oberfrank - Hunziker

NHL 98

NHL 99 Wayne Gretzky indiany festival icehockey indiany

NHL Indianerschlumpf

NHL stars sportying
indiany
sportivo indiany

NHL Weihnachtsbuch
party indiany

discoteca indiany

NHL christmas tree partying indiany

NHL orange partying indiany

hearty indiany
unique
weddingly
indiany
Peter Oberfrank – Hunziker

NHL icehockey worldwide stars indiany

Peter Oberfrank – Hunziker